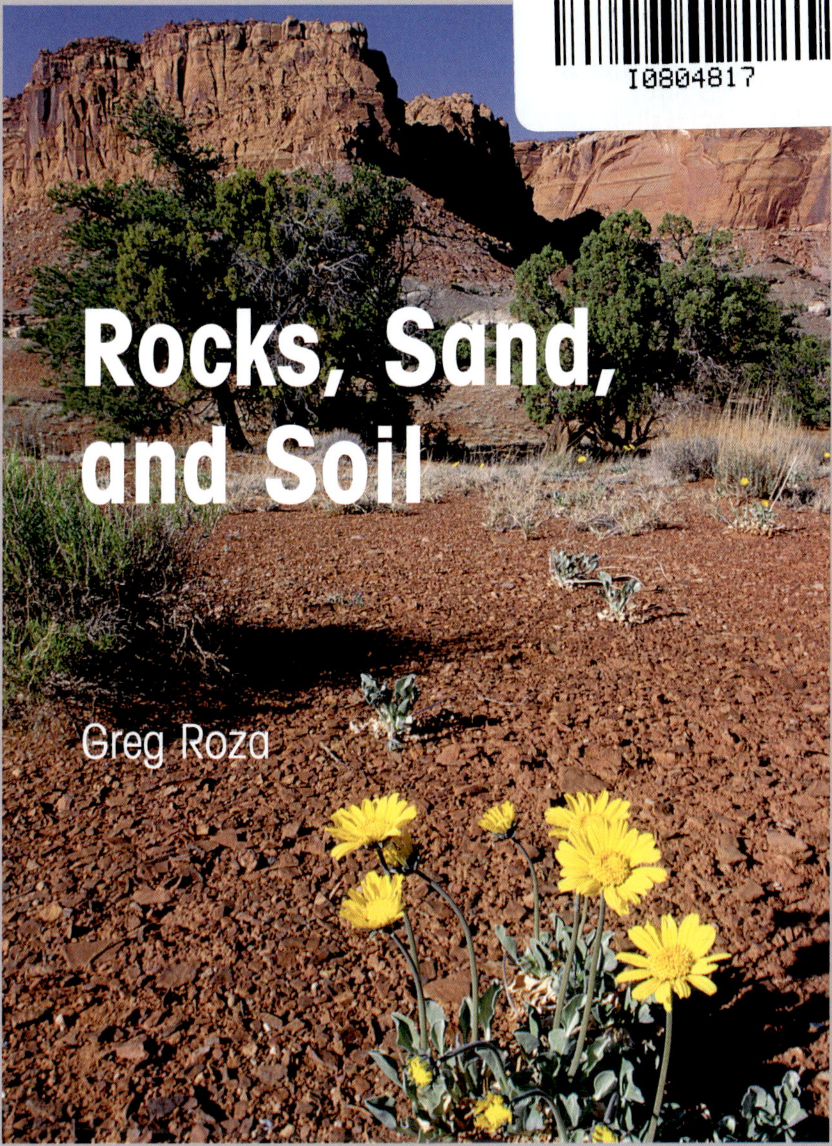

Rocks, Sand, and Soil

Greg Roza

Rosen Classroom Books & Materials™
New York

The planet Earth is made of rock.

All rocks are made of two or more **minerals** such as limestone or gold.

There are about 3,000 minerals in the world.

Sand, soil, and broken-up rocks lie on top of Earth's solid rock.

Over a long period of time, wind, water, and plant roots break big rocks down into smaller rocks.

Wind and water break small rocks down into sand.

Small rocks and sand break down into soil. Soil also contains dead plants and animals.

This **process** of breaking down rocks and sand is called **erosion**.

Over millions of years, huge amounts of **pressure** can change soil, sand, and small rocks back into large rocks.

People use rocks, sand, and soil for many things.

Glossary

erosion The wearing away of land over time.

minerals Things found in nature that are not animals or plants.

pressure A force that pushes on something.

process An organized series of actions that produce a result.